SIMPLE SOLUTIONS TO RUBIK'S MAGIC™

BY

JAMES G. NOURSE

Illustrated by

EDNA McNABNEY
DUSAN KRAJAN
JOE FLORESTAN

BANTAM BOOKS
TORONTO • NEW YORK • LONDON • SYDNEY • AUCKLAND

To Cindy and Tommy

ACKNOWLEDGMENTS
To Jack Looney who does more work than anyone putting these books together.

And to Professor Rubik for his inventiveness.

SIMPLE SOLUTIONS TO RUBIK'S MAGIC™
A Bantam Book / December 1986

ISBN 0-553-26768-X

Published simultaneously in the United States and Canada

Bantam Books are published by Bantam Books, Inc. Its trademark, consisting of
the words "Bantam Books" and the portrayal of a rooster, is Registered in U.S.
Patent and Trademark Office and in other countries. Marca Registrada. Bantam
Books, Inc., 666 Fifth Avenue, New York, New York 10103.

PRINTED IN THE UNITED STATES OF AMERICA

O   0 9 8 7 6 5 4 3 2 1

CONTENTS

ABOUT THIS BOOK

Just when it appeared that the craze for Rubik's Cube had finally quieted to a whisper, the 20th century's master puzzler has come up with another puzzle to entertain and frustrate all those who have finally managed to put their infamous cube away. Professor Rubik's latest invention—Rubik's Magic—has just started on its way to international fame (or infamy). Like all of Prof. Rubik's previous inventions, this is a fascinating puzzle that is not easily solved, even with persistent effort. In addition, this puzzle is also an absorbing and challenging toy, since it can be manipulated into an infinity of remarkable shapes and designs.

For those of you still frustrated by this new puzzle, this book offers a step-by-step solution to get you to the elusive "linked rings." For those of you who have solved it on your own, this book also offers ideas for shapes, designs, and even other puzzles.

Here are some features of this book:

Allows for Error

At the end of each move in the step-by-step solution, there is a section about possible problems, with explanations of what went wrong and what to do.

Simple and Easy to Memorize Moves

Most of the steps in the step-by-step solution (see page 26) are done with the same simple moves in slightly different order. In addition, these moves are designed to be largely independent of the orientation (the way you hold the puzzle). Remember that with Rubik's Cube, if you turn the wrong face or if you turn the correct face the wrong way, all is lost.

Clear and Steady Progress

You can watch the final design take shape with each step in the solution. This helps you be sure that you are making progress as you go along, rather than just relying on what a book tells you.

Cuts Solving Time

How would you like to be able to take a new Rubik's Magic puzzle out of its package and painlessly solve it? This book explains how to do just that.

Independent of Manufacturing Variations

It is possible for puzzles with exactly the same design to be made slightly differently. Any written solution must take this possibility into account or risk frustrating a large number of puzzle owners. The solution given in this book deals fully with this problem.

Why Some Shapes Can't Be Made

This book gives you a method for deciding whether a desired shape *cannot* be made. It is very frustrating to spend considerable time trying to get the puzzle into a desired shape without knowing whether or not the shape is possible.

Many Ideas for Further Fun

In one respect, this puzzle is superior to the famous cube, since it is capable of being put into an infinity of interesting shapes. This feature of the puzzle means you can have endless fun with it, even after you have solved the linked ring puzzle. This book suggests other possible shapes, designs, and even additional puzzles for both the novice and expert.

ABOUT RUBIK'S MAGIC™

Do you remember the old falling-block toy sometimes called "Chinese blocks"? Perhaps 6 blocks are connected with alternating single and double straps. All except the end blocks have straps on both sides. When the top block is turned down so it touches the face of the neighboring block below, a chain reaction occurs, with each block falling in sequence until a new chain is formed. Single straps move between double straps to the neighboring block.

Rubik's Magic can be thought of as a very clever and elaborate design based on the same principle. The puzzle consists of 8 plastic squares connected to each other by very thin filaments, or cords, that rest in grooves cut into the plastic squares. Each square is attached to 2 others by these cords.

The puzzle moves the way it does because of the clever way the cords are wrapped around the plastic squares. There are 16 separate cords holding the 8 squares together (you can verify this if your puzzle falls apart, as these puzzles sometimes do after misuse). The ends of each cord are attached to each other by a small metal clip to form a circle about 5.5 inches in diameter. Pairs of cords cross each other, and where these crossings occur, the cords pass between each other as shown here:

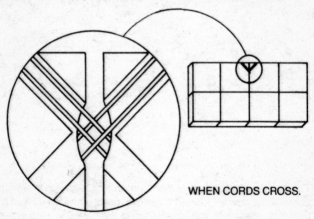

WHEN CORDS CROSS.

The puzzle moves by changes in the relative positions of adjacent squares. Squares are folded over on top of other squares and then pulled up so that different edges are touching when the move is done.

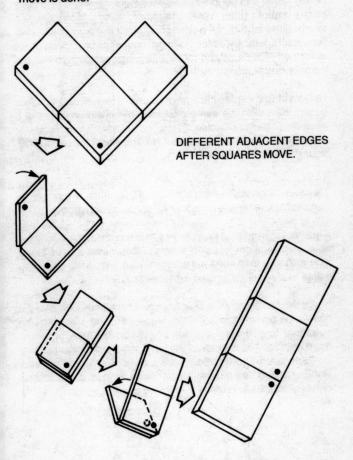

DIFFERENT ADJACENT EDGES AFTER SQUARES MOVE.

This move causes some of the segments of the cords to switch between 2 squares. During the move, parts of the cords "jump" from one square to the other. During this jumping motion the parts of the cords pass between each other in a manner similar to the way the straps on the falling-block toy move.

The puzzle with 8 squares can be thought of as consisting of 4 overlapping sets of 3 squares.

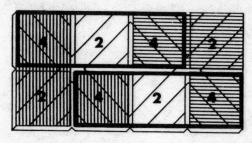

THE 4 GROUPS OF 3 SQUARES AND THE NUMBER OF CORDS PER GROOVE ON EACH SQUARE.

There are 4 cords attaching each set of 3 squares, which means that alternating squares have 4 or 2 cords in each groove.

If you accidentally destroy one of these puzzles, you may be able to salvage one of the 3-square pieces, which can be fun to play with and may serve as a consolation prize for a child who wants to play with your next 8-square puzzle.

Since the entire puzzle is built from smaller pieces in this way, it should be possible to construct larger versions. I wouldn't be surprised to see such puzzles appear as this one becomes more popular. You may recall the large variety of similar puzzles that appeared shortly after Rubik's Cube. Perhaps Professor Rubik will also come up with other ways to wrap cords around different shapes to provide even more challenging puzzles.

TERMINOLOGY

Rubik's Magic is made up of 8 squares connected by very thin cords. Each square has grooves cut into it in which the cords rest. Each square has 2 faces and 4 edges.

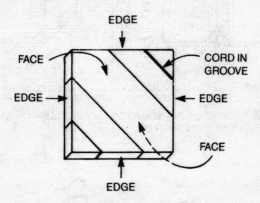

THE PARTS OF A SQUARE.

BASIC MOVES

Rubik's Magic can be changed from any of its shapes to any other by 1 or more moves in which 2 adjacent squares are folded together and then unfolded on a different edge.

The edges of the 2 squares that will become adjacent after the move are the ones on either side of the 2 small pieces of cord shown in the illustration. By looking for these 2 small pieces of cord, you can always tell which way the squares will move.

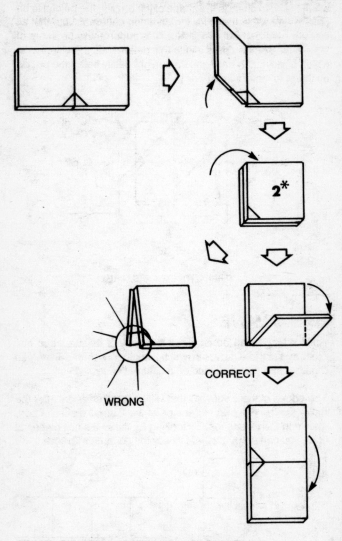

2*

WRONG

CORRECT

CORRECT AND INCORRECT OPENING.

*INDICATES 2 LAYERS OF SQUARES FOR QUICK REFERENCE

Squares can form patterns that you can move in useful ways when trying to change the shape of the puzzle. It is helpful to be able to recognize the following common patterns. Note that all these moves go both ways. Also, it is important to be aware of the position of the cords, since this determines the direction in which a move can be made. You might easily break the puzzle by trying to move it improperly.

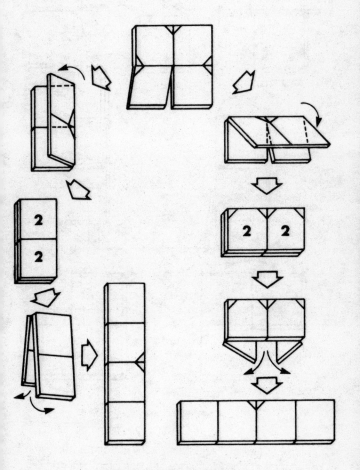

OPEN A 4-SQUARES 2 WAYS.

11

A single square that pops up by itself I call a "flap." Moving flaps is one way to change shapes.

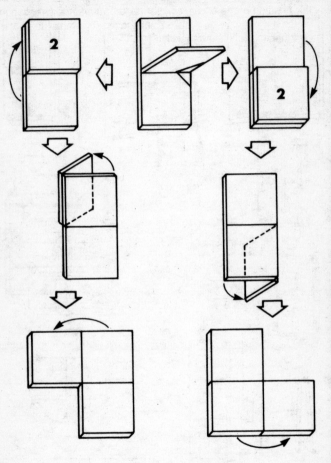

MOVE A FLAP 2 WAYS.

There are 7 ways to move out of a double flap, making it one of the most versatile patterns.

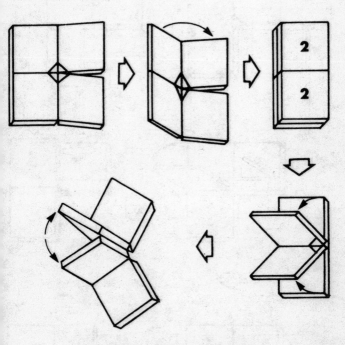

ONE WAY OF OPENING A DOUBLE FLAP.

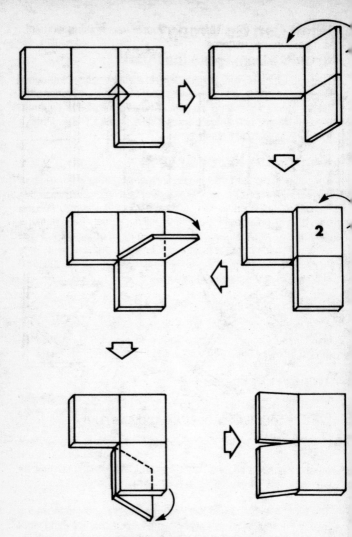

SEQUENCE OF 2-FLAP MOVES.

If all else fails, just try folding and unfolding the puzzle without forcing it too hard. For a change to occur, 2 squares must be touching on 1 face.

What Can Go Wrong?

Avoiding Damage to the Puzzle

The manufacturer has provided several very important sugges-
tions to help you avoid damaging your puzzle. If you ignore this
advice, you risk ending up with a handful of plastic squares,
colored paper, and loose cords. Unlike Rubik's Cube, Rubik's
Magic is not simple to reassemble.

Keeping the Puzzle Aligned

It is also important to follow the manufacturer's suggestion
whenever the puzzle gets slightly out of alignment. When this
happens, 2 adjacent squares will tend to overlap slightly, and the
puzzle in its original 2-by-4 shape will not lie flat. Try pulling the
overlapping squares apart and moving them up and down with
respect to each other. I have found that these puzzles get slightly
looser as they are used, so problems with alignment and
stiffness tend to go away.

Cords out of Grooves

A minor problem can occur when the longer cord segments fall
slightly out of their grooves. When this happens, just gently
nudge the cord back and then jiggle the 2 squares a little bit.

Twisted Cords

Sometimes twists in the cords will accumulate in one place and
prevent the pairs of cords from passing between each other as
they should, which can prevent otherwise permitted moves from
being made. In a normal permitted move the small segments of
cord pairs pass between each other. If there are twists in the
outer pair of cords, this movement of the inner pair may be
blocked, and the squares will not reopen all the way.

The feeling will be much the same as when you try to move the
puzzle improperly. If you ever have trouble accomplishing what
should be a permitted move, you should consider the possibility
that cords are twisted.

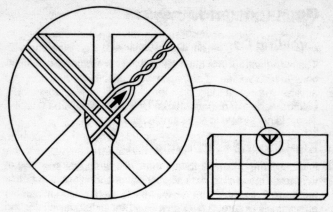

TWISTS IN CORD AT CROSSING.

TWISTS BLOCK MOVEMENT OF CORDS THROUGH EACH OTHER.

To fix the problem you must carefully push the accumulated twisted cords through to the other side of the puzzle.

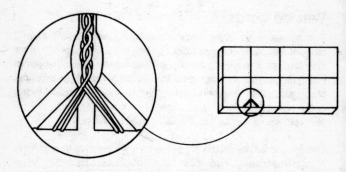

PUSH TWISTS THROUGH TO OTHER SIDE.

This has the effect of putting the twists into the larger cord segments where they can be somewhat dissipated.

Questions and Answers

Whenever I get a new puzzle like this one, besides trying to solve it I like to figure out how complicated it is. What moves? What changes? What stays the same? How difficult is it? And so on.

Can All 8 Squares Be Switched Around?

The answer is that the eight squares can all be moved to any position, but not in all possible ways. In other words, it *is* possible for each of the 8 squares to be on any corner or anywhere in the interior of the original 2-by-4 shape. But if you look carefully at the puzzle, you will notice that each square is always attached to the same 2 neighbors no matter how many times it is moved. In effect, the 8 squares form a necklace held together with the thin cords. This is why the squares *cannot* be moved to all positions *in all possible combinations.*

Can the 8 Squares Be Rotated?

The answer is that all the squares can be rotated, but there are restrictions on the combinations of rotations that can occur. In other words, the design on a square can point in four different directions, but when this changes for one square, it changes for several others at the same time.

Can the Squares Be Turned Over?

The answer is no, unless all 8 squares are flipped. There are 2 sides to the puzzle, as you can see when it is first opened. One side has the design that forms the 3 separate ovals. The other has the design that forms the 3 interlocked ovals of the solution. It is not possible to get a "mixed" design on the 2-by-4 shape.

IMPOSSIBLE DESIGN.

What Shapes Can't Be Made?

One of the first things I tried to do with this puzzle after solving it was to make a flat window shape.

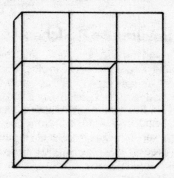

CAN THE WINDOW SHAPE BE MADE?

After considerable unsuccessful effort I decided to try to figure out whether or not it was even possible to make this shape. It turns out to be impossible, and I could have saved myself a lot of wasted effort if I had known this ahead of time. There is enough frustration with these puzzles without trying to do things that are impossible.

I know from experience that I cannot claim that something cannot be done in a puzzle solution book without backing it up, so I will give a brief explanation.

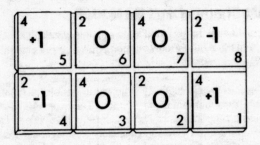

In this illustration, the number in the upper left corner of each square is the number of cords in each groove on the square. The number in the lower right is the number of the square. Starting at number 1 let's travel to all 8 squares and back to number 1. If we make a right turn through a square with 4 cords, let's add 1. If we make a left turn through a square with 4 cords, let's subtract 1. If we make a right turn through a square with 2 cords, let's subtract 1. If we make a left turn through a square with 2 cords, let's add 1. If we go straight, let's add 0. The numbers in the centers of the squares are the values we get by traveling around the square in this way. Notice that they add to 0. Believe it or not, this total must always be 0, no matter how we might change the shape of the puzzle by making moves.

If we do the same calculation on the window shape, we get a total of 4! Therefore, the window shape cannot be made. You can use this method to decide if other shapes can be made. If you find this kind of thing interesting, try to figure out the effect of "flaps" on the method.

How Difficult Is It to Solve?

A quick answer here is that the puzzle is easier than Rubik's Cube, but the many possible shapes make it more interesting to play (or work) with.

One way to gauge difficulty is to try to count the number of possible arrangements and shapes. There are 43 quintillion possible arrangements of Rubik's Cube. In the case of Rubik's Magic, there is no obvious definition of what makes shapes different. Since the puzzle can be moved gradually to make slightly different shapes, it may make sense to just say there are infinitely many shapes possible.

Nevertheless, one way of counting possible shapes is based on the number of right turns, left turns, and flaps—similar to the method used to decide if a shape is possible (see page 18). This method ignores the geometric shape, mirror images, the position of the cords, the design, and whether the shape is turned inside out. There are no more than 1,351 possible shapes, counted this way, and only 59 of these do not have flaps.

An Important Difference

This puzzle is unlike its predecessors in an important way. According to how the puzzle is made, the thin cords can be in a different position relative to the design on the puzzle. This is possible even when puzzles have exactly the same design, and the difference has a serious impact on a written solution. These two illustrations differ only by the position of the cords with respect to the design:

2 POSSIBLE PLACEMENTS OF CORDS WITH RESPECT TO THE ORIGINAL DESIGN.

When you turn over the left 2 squares, the result depends on the location of the cords. This difference is far more subtle than the differences that plagued attempts to provide general solutions for Rubik's Cube and its imitators. For this puzzle, a written solution must take this possible difference into account. The step-by-step solution presented in this book does that.

SOLVING RUBIK'S MAGIC™

When you first get a Rubik's Cube, it is already solved. The objective is to scramble it and then solve it again yourself. At least this way you see the thing solved once, even if you never manage to solve it again. By contrast Rubik's Magic comes out of the box unsolved, and if you wish to see it solved, you have to do it yourself. To solve this puzzle you really have to do 2 things. You must correctly arrange the design so that the chain pieces are linked and you must change the shape of the puzzle.

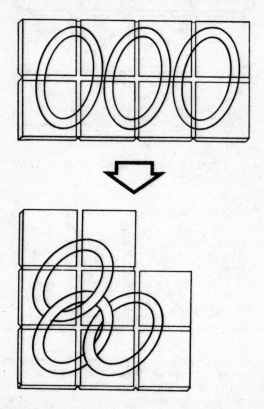

CHANGE THE UNLINKED CHAIN ON THE STARTING 2-BY-4 SHAPE TO THE LINKED CHAIN ON THE FINAL SHAPE, A 3-BY-3 SHAPE MISSING A CORNER.

Overall Strategy

The step-by-step solution given in the next section will allow you to change the puzzle with any design on the 2-by-4 shape to the correct design on the final shape.

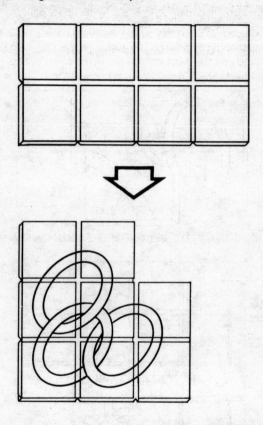

YOU CAN SOLVE THE PUZZLE FROM ANY SCRAMBLED DESIGN.

Methods for converting many other shapes into the 2-by-4 shape without regard to the design are given in the sections following the step-by-step solution.

Summary of the Solution

The solution has 5 main steps:

1. Find the square that will be the center of the design.

2. Position the center square next to the upper right corner of the 2-by-4 shape.

3. Orient the center square so it points the right way.

4. Correctly position neighbors of center square.

5. Change the shape to reveal the solution.

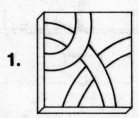

1.

THE SQUARE IN THE CENTER OF THE SOLUTION SHAPE.

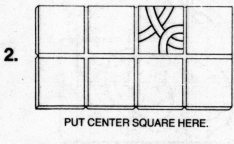

2.

PUT CENTER SQUARE HERE.

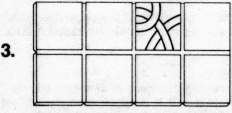

3.

CORRECTLY ORIENT CENTER SQUARE.

4.

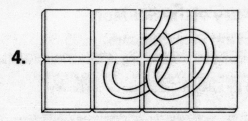

CORRECTLY POSITION NEIGHBORS OF CENTER SQUARE.

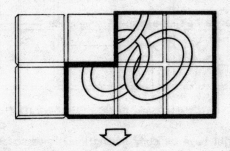

5.

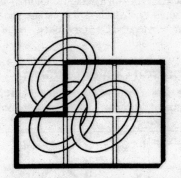

COMPLETE THE DESIGN BY CHANGING THE SHAPE.

Step-by-Step Solution

Step 1: Find Center Square

The center square of the final design is easy to find, since it is the only one with 3 chain pieces on it. Find this square and hold the puzzle so the side with the 3 chain pieces faces you.

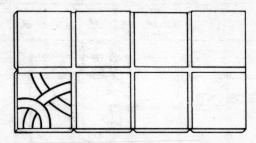

CENTER SQUARE IN INCORRECT POSITION.

You might have difficulty finding the center square if you somehow get a puzzle with a design other than linked chains. If you cannot figure out which is the center square, go to the section called "Moving the Design Around" (page 47).

Step 2: Position Center Square

The objective here is to move the center square into the position next to the upper right corner of the 2-by-4 shape.

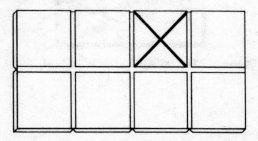

THE CORRECT POSITION FOR THE CENTER SQUARE.

Hold the puzzle with the center square facing you. Now look at the upper right groove on the upper right square. If there is a cord in this groove fold the puzzle like a "W" into 2 stacks of 4 squares. If there is no cord in this groove, fold the puzzle like an "M" into 2 stacks of 4 squares.

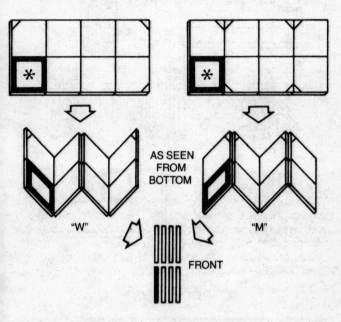

AS SEEN
FROM
BOTTOM

"W"

"M"

FRONT

FOLD INTO 2 STACKS OF 4 SQUARES.

*NOTE: THESE ARE RANDOM POSITIONS FOR THE SQUARE—
INTEREST IS IN UNDERSTANDING THE MOVE ONLY.

Now you can simply pull the squares down on the right side and push them up on the left until the center square is in the correct position. When you are done with this shuffling, simply reopen the puzzle to the 2-by-4 shape.

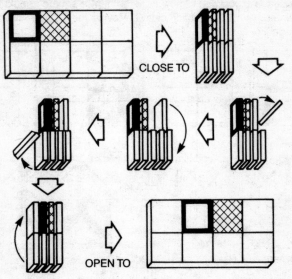

CLOSE TO

OPEN TO

MOVE SQUARES IN STACKS UNTIL THE CENTER SQUARE IS IN THE CORRECT POSITION.

■ PROBLEMS? ■

1. You have the 2 stacks of 4 squares, but when you pull on squares they are stuck. To resolve this, unfold the stacks until you get the 2-by-4 shape and then refold the opposite way. In other words if it unfolds like a "W," refold it like an "M."

2. The squares pull down most of the way but get stuck at the end. This is probably caused by twists in the cords. Look at the section called "Twisted Cords" (page 15).

Step 3: Orient Center Square

Now you must turn the center square until it points the way it is supposed to in the solution design. If your puzzle has a different design and you don't know how the center square should be pointed, go to the section called "Moving the Design Around" (page 47).

CORRECT POSITION AND ORIENTATION OF CENTER SQUARE.

You can rotate this square one-quarter turn to the right by doing the following.

3A. First hold the puzzle so that the side *without* cords in the corners faces you. Now do this sequence of moves.

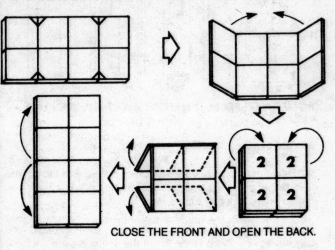

CLOSE THE FRONT AND OPEN THE BACK.

Let's call this the "close front, open back" move.

3B. Now hold the puzzle so the side *with* cords in the corners faces you. Then do this sequence of moves.

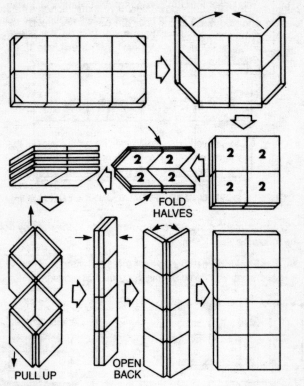

FOLD HALVES

PULL UP

OPEN BACK

CLOSE TWICE FROM THE FRONT AND THEN OPEN LIKE AN ACCORDION.

Let's call this the "close front, accordion" move.

3C. Now hold the puzzle so the center square is in the square next to the upper right corner. You will notice that it has been rotated one-quarter turn clockwise.

Repeat step 3 until the center square is correctly oriented. You may have to do this 3 times to get the center square correctly oriented.

SHORTCUT

You can rotate the center square counterclockwise (to the left) by doing the reverse sequence, first 3B and then 3A. This means you first do the "close front, accordion" move and then the "close front, open back" move.

■ PROBLEMS? ■

1. You have folded the puzzle from the front but the rest of either move 3A or move 3B won't work. This probably means that you were holding the puzzle incorrectly to start. Reopen the puzzle from the front and try again after checking the position of the cords.

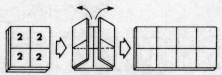

REOPEN FROM FRONT.

2. One of the moves gets stuck when nearly complete. Check the section called "Twisted Cords" (page 15).

3. The center square is in one of these corners.

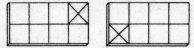

IS THE CENTER SQUARE IN ONE OF THESE CORNERS?

This means you did just one of 3A or 3B but not both. Do step 3A and continue with the rest of step 3.

4. The center square is elsewhere. Go back to step 2.

Step 4: Position Neighbors of Center Square

Look at the squares to the right of and below the center square. Does the design line up as in figure A? If so, you can skip this step and go to step 5; otherwise, continue with step 4.

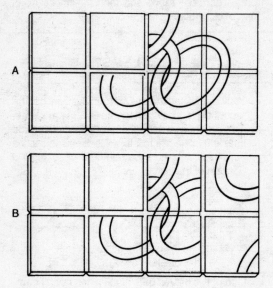

WHICH OF THESE DOES YOUR PUZZLE LOOK LIKE? A. B.

4A. If the side with the center square has cords in the corners, do these moves:

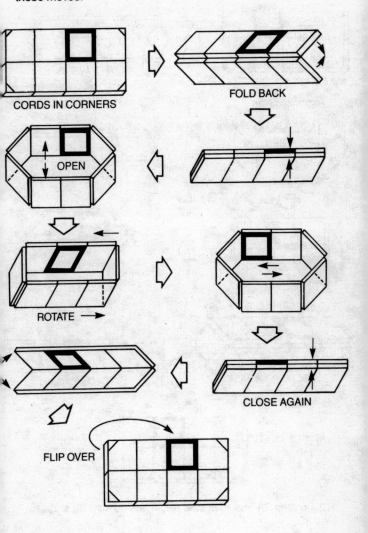

CORDS IN CORNERS

FOLD BACK

OPEN

ROTATE ➡

CLOSE AGAIN

FLIP OVER

Now go to step 4C.

4B. If there are no cords in the corners do these moves:

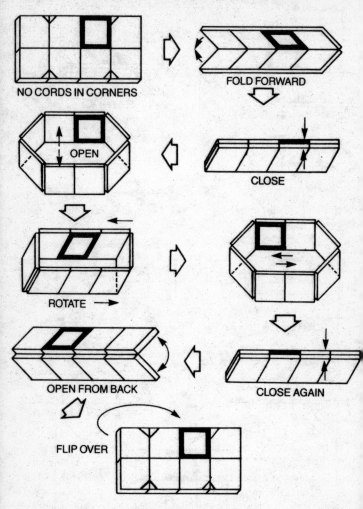

NO CORDS IN CORNERS

FOLD FORWARD

OPEN

CLOSE

ROTATE →

CLOSE AGAIN

OPEN FROM BACK

FLIP OVER

4C. Do step 3A and then step 3B. Again do step 3A and then step 3B.

If the design now lines up, go on to step 5.

1. If the moves in step 4A or step 4B won't go and the puzzle looks like this,

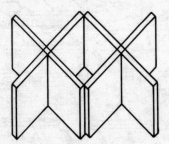

DOES IT LOOK LIKE THIS?

Unfold it from either the front or the back (whichever works) and repeat step 4A, making sure you check for the cords in the corners.

2. If any move goes almost all the way and then gets stuck, check the section "Twisted Cords" (page 15).

3. If the center square ends up in either of these corners,

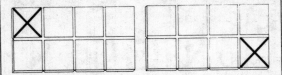

IS THE CENTER SQUARE IN ONE OF THESE POSITIONS?

then do the sequence of moves on the next page: Be sure to note whether there are cords in the corners.

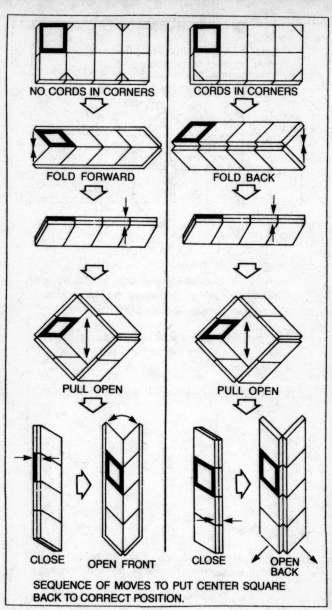

NO CORDS IN CORNERS   CORDS IN CORNERS

FOLD FORWARD   FOLD BACK

PULL OPEN   PULL OPEN

CLOSE   OPEN FRONT   CLOSE   OPEN BACK

SEQUENCE OF MOVES TO PUT CENTER SQUARE
BACK TO CORRECT POSITION.

Now check the orientation of the center square.
If it is incorrect, go back to step 3.

4. If the center square is in either of these corners,

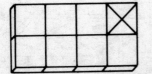 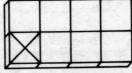

IS THE CENTER SQUARE IN ONE OF THESE
POSITIONS?

go back to problem number 3 in step 3 and
continue with step 3.

Step 5: Change to the Solution Shape

If there are cords in the corners of the puzzle when the center square is facing you, do step 5A. If there are no cords in the corners, do step 5B.

5A. Do the following sequence of moves.

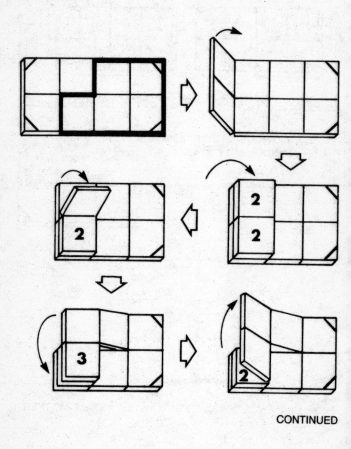

CONTINUED

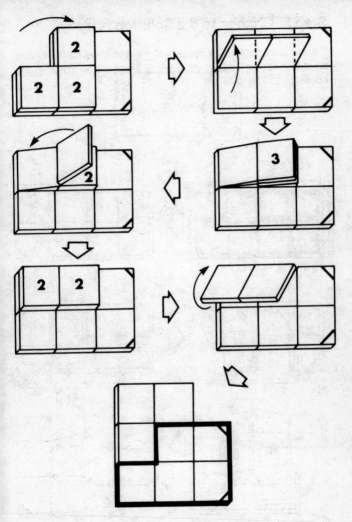

FINAL SEQUENCE OF MOVES TO SOLUTION. NOTE THAT THE 5 OUTLINED SQUARES STAY TOGETHER.

Now go to step 5C.

5B. Do the following sequence of moves. Be particularly careful to turn the puzzle over correctly.

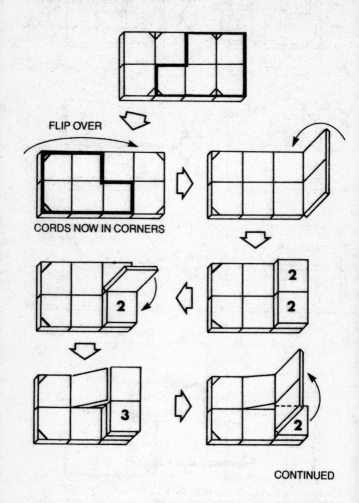

FLIP OVER

CORDS NOW IN CORNERS

CONTINUED

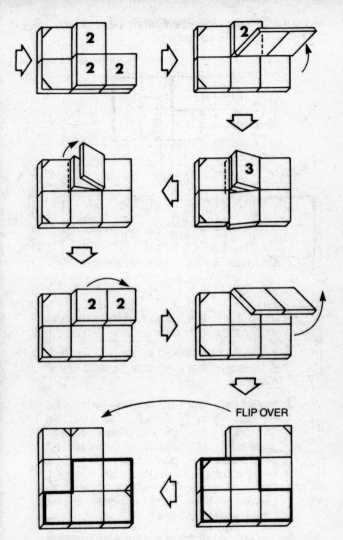

FLIP OVER

ALTERNATIVE FINAL SEQUENCE OF MOVES. NOTE THAT THE 5 OUTLINED SQUARES STAY TOGETHER.

5C. Congratulations! You are done!

■ PROBLEMS? ■

1. If the first moves in step 5 won't go and the puzzle is in shape A or shape B,

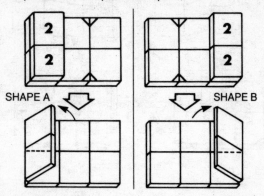

SHAPE A   SHAPE B

IF THE PUZZLE IS IN THIS SHAPE, UNFOLD IT TO THE STARTING SHAPE.

unfold it and repeat step 5, making sure you check for the cords in the corners.

2. If a move goes almost all the way and then gets stuck, check the section "Twisted Cords" (page 15).

3. You got the new shape, but the design is wrong. Carefully reverse the steps you did in either step 5A or 5B, and check the orientation of the center piece and its neighbors. If the center piece is oriented correctly, go back to step 4. If the center square is oriented incorrectly, go back to step 3. If you don't know how it should be oriented, go to the section called "Moving the Design Around" (page 47).

4. You got one of these shapes with 3 squares stacked on the corner. The 2 loose flaps are on the top.

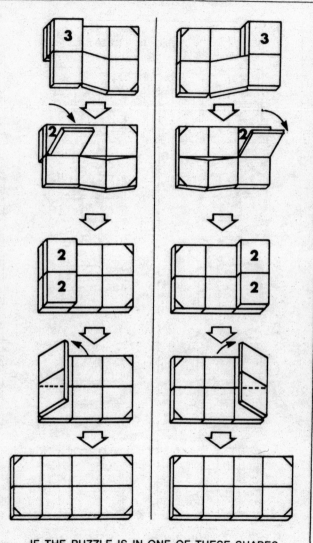

IF THE PUZZLE IS IN ONE OF THESE SHAPES,
CHANGE IT TO THE STARTING SHAPE.

5. You got one of these shapes with three squares stacked on the corner. The 2 loose flaps are on the bottom.

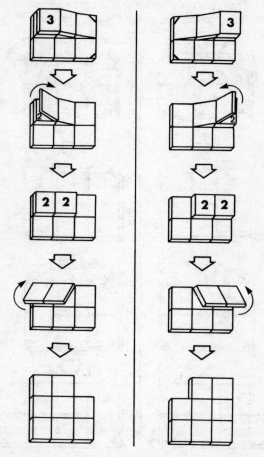

IF THE PUZZLE IS IN ONE OF THESE SHAPES, CHANGE TO THE SOLUTION SHAPE. IF THE DESIGN IS WRONG, SEE PROBLEM 3 ABOVE.

Fast out of the Box!

Here is a method of quickly solving the puzzle from the 3-oval design. This will not necessarily work if you start from another design.

If there are no cords in the corners of the puzzle when the 3-oval design is facing you,

STARTING DESIGN WITH NO CORDS IN THE OUTER CORNERS OF THE PUZZLE.

then do the sequence of moves in step 4B, followed by the sequence of moves in step 3A. Hold your puzzle so it looks like this:

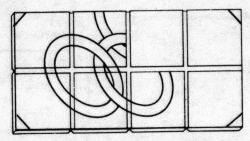

PARTIALLY COMPLETED DESIGN IS THE STARTING POINT FOR FINAL SEQUENCE OF MOVES. THE DESIGN ON ONLY 5 SQUARES IS SHOWN.

Then do the sequence of moves in step 5B without the initial flip. You can get back and forth between the starting shape and the solution shape by reversing these steps.

If there are cords in the corners of the puzzle when the 3-oval design is facing you,

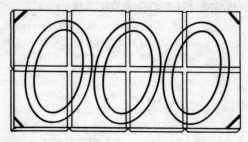

STARTING DESIGN WITH CORDS IN THE OUTER CORNERS OF THE PUZZLE.

then do the sequence of moves in step 4A, followed by the sequence of moves in step 3A. Hold your puzzle so it looks like this:

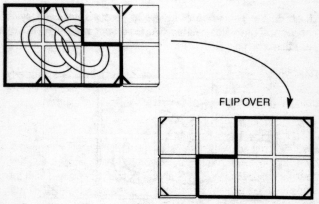

FLIP OVER

FLIP THE PARTIALLY COMPLETED DESIGN BEFORE DOING THE FINAL SEQUENCE OF MOVES. THE DESIGN ON ONLY 5 SQUARES IS SHOWN.

Then flip it over as indicated and do the sequence of moves in step 5A. You can get back and forth between the starting shape and the solution shape by reversing these steps.

MORE ABOUT RUBIK'S MAGIC

Moving the Design Around

Once you have learned to solve the puzzle, you can change the design that appears on both the starting 2-by-4 shape and the solution shape. You might do this if you want to see what other designs look like, or perhaps you didn't know what the final design is supposed to be before you tried to solve the puzzle.

To change the design, so you don't keep seeing the same one over and over again, just follow the steps of the solution in this way:

1. At step 1 make a different choice for the center square each time.

2. At step 3, try all 4 possible orientations for the center square. This means you do step 3 a total of 4 times for each time you do steps 1 and 2.

3. At step 4, try both possible arrangements of the neighbors of the center square. This means you will do step 4 twice for each time you do step 3.

Remember that after step 4, 5 of the squares are properly oriented. You can therefore see most of the final design without doing step 5. Check to see if the design lines up.

Changing to the 2-by-4 Shape

If your puzzle is currently in a shape other than the original 2-by-4 shape (and these puzzles often are!), you will need to change it back to the 2-by-4 shape before proceeding with the step-by-step solution. You need not concern yourself at all with the design on the squares at this stage.

The objective here is to manipulate the puzzle into a "flat" shape that looks like one of these:

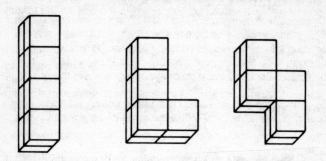

THREE FLAT SHAPES, WHICH LOOK LIKE THE LETTERS I, L, AND S. EACH SQUARE REPRESENTS A STACK OF 2 SQUARES.

Once you have gotten your puzzle into one of the flat shapes, look in the section "Flat Shapes" (see page 49) to see which one it is. Corresponding to each shape, is a sequence of moves that either converts it to the 2-by-4 shape or converts it to some other shape that can be converted to the 2-by-4 shape.

Notation

Here is an example of one of the flat shapes:

HINGE ON TOP   2 POSSIBILITIES   HINGE ON RIGHT

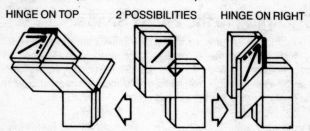

ONE OF THE S SHAPES, SHOWING THE CONNECTIONS OF ONE SQUARE ON THE UPPER LAYER TO THE ONE ON THE LOWER LAYER.

The squares with arrows are the most important. The shaft of the arrow indicates the direction of the cords on the square, and the point of the arrow indicates the 2 edges at which the square on the upper layer can be connected to the one on the lower layer.

Be sure you have chosen the proper flat shape before attempting the corresponding sequence of moves. If you make a mistake and choose the wrong flat shape, the moves will either not work at all or will convert the puzzle into some shape other than the one indicated. It is sometimes difficult to see the thin cords, but their position is very important: some shapes, identical except for the position of the cords, are changed by very different moves.

Hints

1. Always be sure to check the positions of the cords very carefully. If a move doesn't work, recheck the positions of the cords and the edges at which the top and bottom squares are attached. If the move still doesn't work, read the section "Twisted Cords" (page 15).

2. Make sure you hold the flat shape so the letter shape matches one of those in the section **exactly.** In the case of the S shape in the illustration above, make sure the inner corner with 3 cords is the upper one.

3. If you are having trouble getting the puzzle into one of the flat shapes, look at the section "Basic Moves" (page 9). Look for parts of the puzzle that form the patterns of squares illustrated in this section. Also try sequences of opening and closing the puzzle to make various stacked shapes, and try changing the number of squares in a stack.

Flat Shapes

Once you have gotten your puzzle into one of the 3 flat shapes, find it on this list and do the sequence of moves indicated. Be sure to hold your puzzle so the cords and edges attaching the upper squares to the lower ones are as indicated in the illustrations. Sequences of moves shown elsewhere in this book can be used to convert some other shapes back to the original 2-by-4 shape. For example, you may get your puzzle into the solution shape with the design incorrect. In this case, do the sequence of moves in step 5A in reverse.

You can get the puzzle into one of these flat shapes by doing the sequences in reverse.

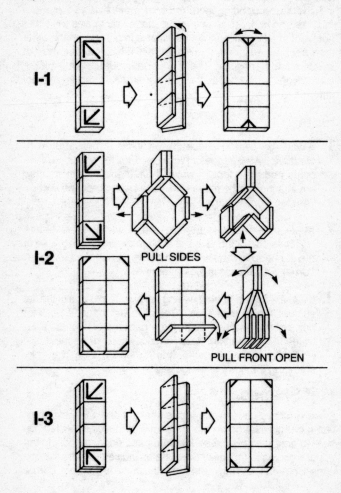

I-1

I-2

PULL SIDES

PULL FRONT OPEN

I-3

S-1

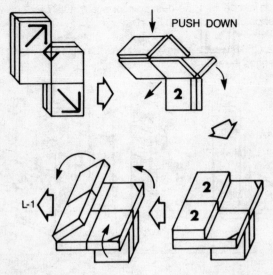

PUSH DOWN

2

2
2

L-1

S-2

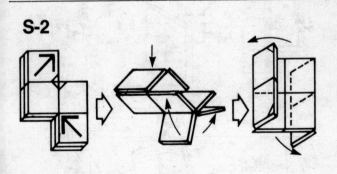

S-3

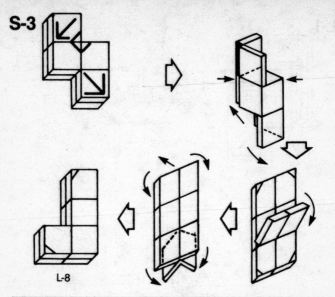

L-8

S-4

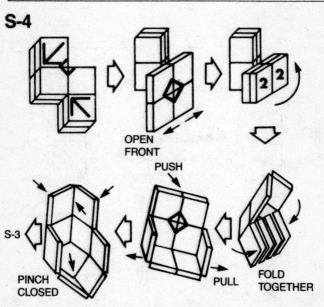

OPEN FRONT

PUSH

FOLD TOGETHER

PULL

PINCH CLOSED

S-3

52

L-1

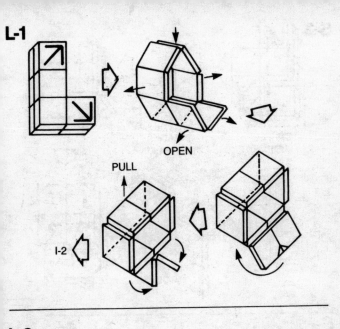

OPEN

PULL

I-2

L-2

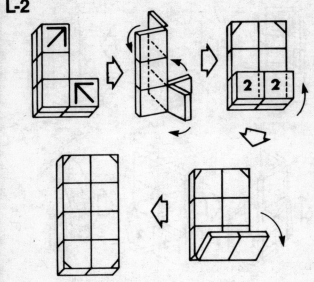

2 **2**

53

L-3

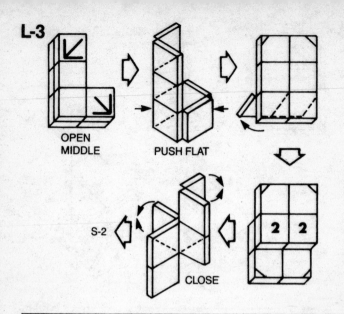

OPEN MIDDLE

PUSH FLAT

S-2

CLOSE

2 2

L-4

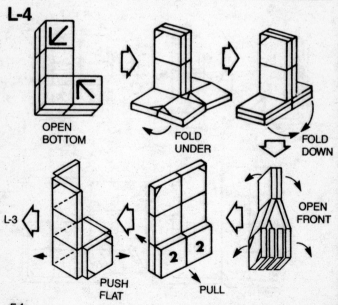

OPEN BOTTOM

FOLD UNDER

FOLD DOWN

OPEN FRONT

L-3

PUSH FLAT

PULL

2 2

54

L-5

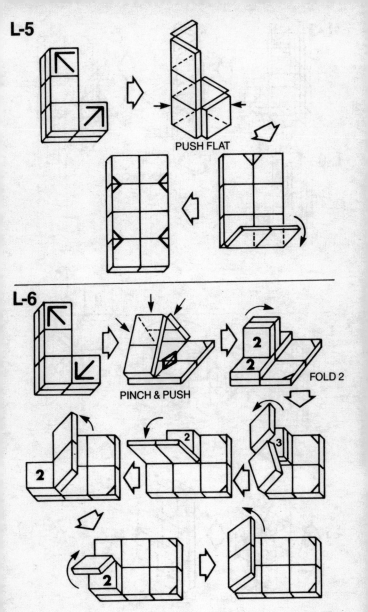

PUSH FLAT

L-6

PINCH & PUSH

FOLD 2

2

2

2

3

2

2

55

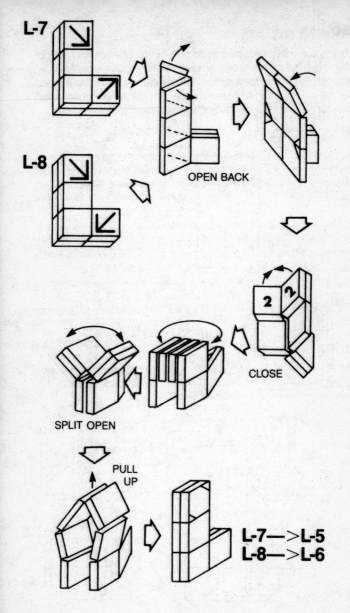

L-7

L-8

OPEN BACK

CLOSE

SPLIT OPEN

PULL UP

L-7—>L-5
L-8—>L-6

56

More Fun

There is much more you can do with this puzzle besides linking the rings. In fact I think of this latest Rubik creation more as a toy with endless possibilities than just as a puzzle. Here are 5 ideas for having more fun with your puzzle. The 5 increase in difficulty, so that number 1 is the easiest and number 5 is the hardest.

1. More Designs

A. Start with the original 3-oval design. Now try the sequence of moves given for problem number 3 in step 4 of the step-by-step solution. Be sure about the position of the cords. See how the ovals move?

B. Start again with the original 3-oval design. Do the sequence of moves in step 3A of the step-by-step solution. Now do the moves in A, above. The design will be just one oval on its side.

C. Look at the design you get after you do the first 2 sequences of moves in the section "Fast out of the Box" (page 45). Now do the sequence of moves in A, above. The 2 ovals bounce up and down.

2. More Shapes

Do not concern yourself with the design in this section. You are going to make interesting shapes starting from some of the "L" shapes.

A. Star

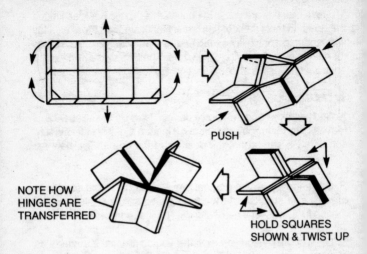

PUSH

NOTE HOW HINGES ARE TRANSFERRED

HOLD SQUARES SHOWN & TWIST UP

MAKE AN EIGHT-POINTED STAR.

B. Building

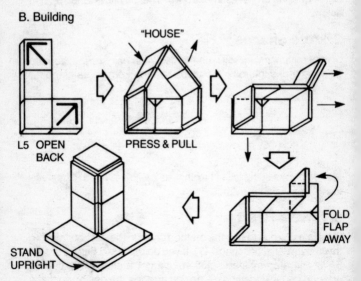

L5 OPEN BACK

"HOUSE"

PRESS & PULL

FOLD FLAP AWAY

STAND UPRIGHT

MAKE A HIGHRISE BUILDING FROM A HOUSE.

C. Orange crate

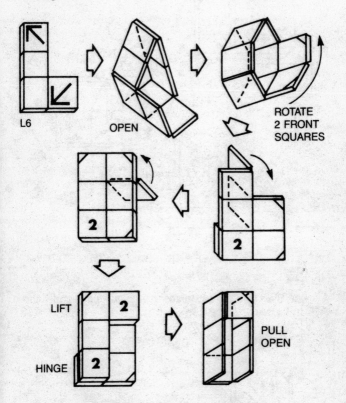

L6

OPEN

ROTATE
2 FRONT
SQUARES

LIFT

HINGE

PULL
OPEN

MAKE AN ORANGE CRATE WITHOUT ORANGES.

Many shapes in the list of flat shapes can be opened to interesting 3-dimensional shapes.

3. Have a Heart

Here is a chance to use the method given in the section "Moving the Design Around" (page 47). If you do the first 3 moves in step 5A of the step-by-step solution, you get a shape that can be opened into a kind of box. Can you arrange the design so that a heart appears inside the box?

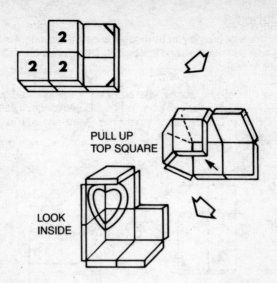

PULL UP
TOP SQUARE

LOOK
INSIDE

UNFOLD THE FLAT SHAPE INTO A BOX. CAN YOU DO IT WITH HEART?

Answer: Start with the 3-oval design and make design 1A above. Hold it like this:

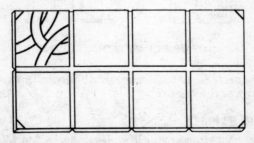

HOLD PUZZLE WITH THIS SQUARE IN THE UPPER LEFT CORNER AND THE CORDS AS SHOWN.

Now do the first 3 moves in step 5A and open to reveal a heart.

4. Cubes

Since this new puzzle can be thought of as a descendant of the cube, let's see if we can find a cube in it. These are more difficult shapes to make.

This is my favorite shape, the cube on a stand. Start with the 2-by-4 shape in any design and do this sequence. If you're stuck, do the L-6 sequence in reverse (see page 55) to get L-8 (see page 56).

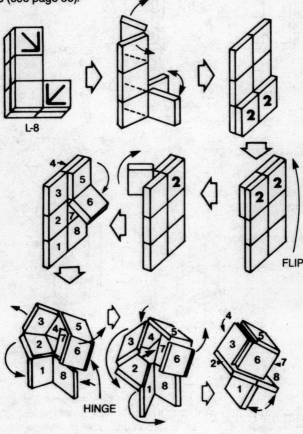

CUBE PROMINENTLY DISPLAYED ON ITS OWN STAND.

Can you make another cube from the solution shape?

Answer: Do this sequence. This cube also converts into a basket.

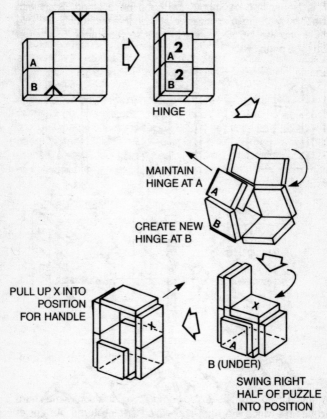

HINGE

MAINTAIN HINGE AT A

CREATE NEW HINGE AT B

PULL UP X INTO POSITION FOR HANDLE

B (UNDER)

SWING RIGHT HALF OF PUZZLE INTO POSITION

CUBE THAT TURNS INTO A BASKET.

Now try to design your own cube. There are more cube shapes possible than the ones here. It helps to think about the arrangement of squares that are folded into a cube, as if you were to make a cube out of paper squares cut from one piece of paper. The 6 squares could be attached together only in certain ways.

5. Make the Most Shapes

Now for the hardest challenge. In the section "How Difficult Is It to Solve?" (Page 20), I said that only 59 different shapes are possible if you consider only the number of right and left turns and do not allow flaps. How many of these 59 shapes can you make? Refer to the section "What Shapes Can't Be Made?" (page 18) to get an explanation of how to determine the right and left turns. Each shape can be classified by its sequence of turns and straight pieces. The original 2-by-4 shape has 4 right turns and 4 straight pieces in the sequence RSSRRSSR.

It is important to know when 2 shapes are the same according to this notation. You can start with any square and go in either direction. When you get the final sequence of 8 letters you can change all the R's to L's and vice-versa. Thus, many of these RLS sequences are effectively the same. Also, shapes that are very different in appearance can give the same sequence of RLS symbols.

DARKENED EDGES SHOW 2 SQUARES CONNECTED (HINGED).

Many of these shapes are so complex that it is sometimes hard to decide which are right and which are left turns. An easier method is to use a puzzle with numbers on it, like the illustration above. Simply follow the sequence of 8 squares around and look at the darkened edges. Write down the number that is next to each of these 8 darkened edges. Using the illustration, you would get 02010201. Each square has 2 darkened edges and will therefore have 2 numbers associated with it. Now follow these rules:

1. If the numbers go 0-2, 2-0, 1-3, 3-1, then there is no turn at this square, so it is straight.

2. If the numbers go 0-1, 1-2, 2-3, 3-0 and the square has 4 cords, it is a left turn. If the square has 2 cords, it is a right turn.

3. If the numbers go 1-0, 2-1, 3-2, 0-3 and the square has 4 cords, it is a right turn. If the square has 2 cords, it is left turn.

4. If 2 consecutive numbers are the same, the shape has a flap and doesn't count.

I have so far been able to make 51 shapes this way. Can you do better? Be careful not to include shapes with RLS sequences that are effectively the same.